S I S

Myth and Truth

Katrin Unterreiner

S I S I

Myth and Truth

Translated by Neil Radford

CHRISTIAN BRANDSTÄTTER VERLAG
WIEN–MÜNCHEN

April 2004 saw the opening of the museum entitled »Sisi – Myth and Truth« in the Wiener Hofburg and has been a hit with the public since.

Prof. Rolf Langenfass, international stage and costume designer in Vienna, planned, devised and fashioned – i. e. staged this museum artistically. The dramaturgical direction of the museum was adopted structurally in this book by Katrin Unterreiner who, as curator of the museum, worked closely with Rolf Langenfass.

TABLE OF CONTENTS

Foreword

There has hardly ever been a monarch stylised post-humously to such iconic status as empress Elisabeth. But »Sissi« did not become an internationally marketed product, with a romanticised biography and entwined by legend, until long after her death. It certainly does not accurately represent empress Elisabeth, for whom comparatively little interest was shown during her lifetime.

An attempt was made in 2004, in the newly opened Sisi Museum in the emperor apartments of the Viennese imperial palace, to dispel this myth of historical reality and to set out in search of the empress aloof of legend and cliché. The results of the extensive research for the Sisi Museum are presented here in book format and throw new light on the eccentric empress. The assassination plays a crucial role in the emergence of the Elisabeth icon. The most important chapters in the life of Elisabeth from that point on, in particular developments of her persona, are discussed: Her engagement in Ischl, her supposed love marriage to emperor Franz Joseph, her role as empress of Austria, her revolt against court life and increasingly running away from herself manifesting itself in a beauty cult, slimming fanaticism, high-performance sport and lyrical poetry. This book accompanies the restless empress on her journeys, up to her assassination in Geneva. Individual subject areas are prefixed with quotes taken directly

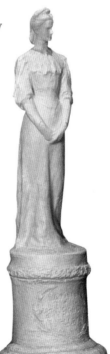

Left: Design by Edmund Hellmer for the Elisabeth memorial in Hellbrunn, Salzburg.

Opposite page: Elisabeth of Austria, posthumous portrait by Gyula Benczúr, 1899.

from Elisabeth's literary remains so as to better understand Elisabeth's train of thought, to allow her to »speak« for herself . In addition there are contributions from people within her closest circle, amongst them her ladies-in-waiting Marie Festetics and Irma Sztáray, her daughter Marie Valerie and her Greek reader Constantin Christomanos, who paint as intuitive and authentic a picture as possible of the private Elisabeth. For the first time, and with the help of new sources such as the diary of her butler Leopold Alram, who accompanied the empress over many years on her journeys, we have the opportunity to meet Elisabeth herself. This book highlights just how important it is to challenge clichés in order to arrive ultimately at the truth.

I would like to express my thanks to everyone who supported me with this book, especially Michael Wohlfart and Monika Levay for their valuable input and our discussions about empress Elisabeth.

I would like to extend my thanks to Professor Rolf Langenfass for his cooperation in making the Sisi Museum a reality.

Above: Elisabeth as fiancée at the age of sixteen; anonymous painting, 1853/54.

Opposite page: Memorial page for empress Elisabeth with some incorrect dating.

Unsere Kaiserin
in ihren verschiedenen Lebensaltern.

Verlag von J. H. Spitzer, Wien, Czerningasse 21.
Mit Vorbehalt der Nachbildung und Vervielfältigung.

THE CREATION OF A MYTH

Above: Benefit stamp
Viribus Unitis;
design by Joseph Urban,
engraving by Ferdinand
Schirnböck, 1914.

Opposite page:
Commemorative
photograph of empress
Elisabeth; Carl Pietzner's
retouched posthumous
version of the photograph
by Ludwig Angerer
from 1868/69.

DEATH

On 10th September 1898 Europe was shocked by the news: Empress Elisabeth of Austria assassinated! Elisabeth's tragic death was the end of an emotional, troubled and often misunderstood life of a remarkable person. Today, »Sisi« is associated with the memory of a gorgeous, unceremonious and perhaps extravagant empress – almost everybody visualises the delightfully young Romy Schneider in the famed »Sissi«-films from the 1950s. This of course has little in common with the real empress Elisabeth. Just how did this »Sisi« myth arise? How did an enthusiast young girl turn into somebody so frustrated, perplexed, and would rather be dead? How did this person, for whom contemporaries had little time, become such an icon long after her death? The assassination of the empress, the tragic end of a troubled life, was certainly a contributing factor in the creation of this myth, but which was already being cultivated by Elisabeth's unconventional lifestyle.

Above: Empress Elisabeth's »Death mask«; Franz Matsch, around 1900.

Opposite page:
Top: Empress Elisabeth's coffin is carried from the Hotel Beau Rivage in Geneva.

Bottom: Memorial keepsake of empress Elisabeth.

But mournfully I spread
my wide, white wings,
and return home to the fairy kingdom;
Nothing shall bring me back again …
To my child, 1888

THE ICON

Above: »The icon«,
Sisi Museum, Production
by Rolf Langenfass.

Opposite page:
Top: What is thought to
be the last photograph of
the empress; Ludwig
Angerer, 1868/69.

Bottom: Porcelain mug
with portrait of Elisabeth;
historical collector's item.

*The memory of this ruler, so enthusiastic about beauty
and so full of sorrow, will live on in history as a
resplendent and poetical image. And that she did not
die in bed, through illness or of old age,
but rather collapsed dead at the hands of
a fanatical madman, just as she had set foot
on the landing stage for a new journey into wondrous
surroundings she loved so much, it will, as
harrowingly sad it may be, so despicable the deed
to blame for it, it will accompany this image
with tragic charm.
You rise above the gloom of everyday life
for all time, a figure in the luminous darkness
Elisabeth of Austria!*

Bertha von Suttner

How was Elisabeth actually viewed by her contemporaries? The newspaper cuttings showed quite clearly that during her lifetime Elisabeth was not the beautiful, popular and acclaimed empress who filled the front pages of the newspapers. The fact of the matter is that there were very few reports about Elisabeth, who withdraws from her public role as empress very early and was seldom in Vienna during the last few years of her life. Little is known about the life of the empress and she is seen only occasionally at public occasions, putting her unsociableness down to worsening health. Since newspapers published within the monarchy are also subject to strict censorship in matters regarding the royal household, critical reports of the empress are unlikely to appear. It is Emperor Franz Joseph who occupies a far more important role here – as the »good old emperor« he has a place in his people's heart and is universally liked. This is borne out by the public reaction following the death of the successor to the throne, in which sympathy was most notably expressed for the emperor as the victim of yet another heavy blow of fate. In aristocratic circles considerably more pressure is brought to bear on the indifference of the empress to fulfil her monarchal responsibilities, instead of

Right: Remembrance page of empress Elisabeth with view of Elisabeth's »Odysseus island« near Corfu.

Opposite page: Souvenir of empress Elisabeth; painted on silk from the last photograph by Ludwig Angerer, 1868/69.

putting her personal interests first. The situation changes dramatically after the tragic murder of the empress when it is realized that the tale of the young, shy princess is very marketable - suddenly becoming empress and, as a freedom-loving person, adhering to the rigid hierarchies and court ceremonial, developing into a beautiful and confident woman, escaping the gilded cage and beginning to live her own independent life, still unhappy and being tragically killed. And so Elisabeth is posthumously stylised as a revered, selfless and well-meaning empress. A critical debate about her ambivalent personality, her egocentricity and egomania is left out completely, thus establishing a false image.

After a several week absence from Vienna, the empress arrived in Penzing yesterday morning, accompanied by the Grand Master of the Household, Count Bellegarde, the lady-in-waiting countess Sztáray and a further small entourage from Bad Schwalbach. About 15 minutes before the arrival of the train the monarch drove up to the station building accompanied by the Adjutant-General and went up to the platform. When the train stopped, the Kaiser approached the imperial salon carriage, whereupon the empress came into view on the little steps. The monarch has clearly recovered during her stay in Kissingen and Schwalbach; she carried a plain black travel case and a small round black hat with veil flipped back. The king helps the empress, welcomes her sincerely and then, and after having greeted her travelling companions, drives off sitting at the side of the empress in an open equipage to Lainzer Castle, where the empress plans to spend several weeks.

Agramer Zeitung 10th July 1879

In recognition of the empress's stay in Venice in winter 1861/62 the »Wiener Bote« reports from Venice:

Accompanied by fine weather, the Queen of the Adriatic welcomed the empress on the morning of 26th November. The reception was not so much rapturous as more sincere, as to be predicted such was the liking for the empress who had won over hearts, and to which the call of the local authorities to the people could have contributed.

The Morgenpost reports the stay of the empress in Sassetôt as:

The positive improvement in the health of her majesty the empress continues without problem. Her condition has improved somewhat. After being summoned by telegraph, the head of the railway, Ritter von Klauda, arrived in Vienna; he is to assume control of the imperial train, with which the empress will leave Normandy. The empress will stay in Paris for two days, not in the Austrian embassy however, but in the »Bristol« hotel.

Morgenpost, 21st September 1875

During Elisabeth's lifetime little public interest was shown in the reclusive and rather »eccentric« empress – it was not until after her death that the commercial possibilities of the image of the beautiful and unhappy empress who had lost her life so tragically were recognised. Soon there was a rash of memorial pictures, memorial coins and other memorabilia of the empress in circulation. Significantly it was not an authentic portrait that was used as a master for these quickly sought-after collector's items, but rather a fantasy figure created by using photomontage and retouche, with little association with Elisabeth. The master used was the last studio photograph of Elisabeth which Ludwig Angerer had made in 1868/69, when Elisabeth was in her early 30s. By using retouche, Elisabeth aged discreetly, clothing and hairstyle were adapted in accordance with the fashion and the picture of an empress that had never existed as such was complete.

During the same period in the 1920s the first serialised novel »Empress Elisabeth« appeared on the market. These novels form the basis for all later exploitations of the story of the empress. For the first time mention was made of her romantic and loving marriage, which, at least as far as Elisabeth was

Die Trauung in der Wiener Hofkirche

Die junge Kaiserin

Das junge Kaiser-Brautpaar

concerned, was never the case. For the first time, Elisabeth is also depicted as a celebrated, popular empress, adored by her people, which was also far from the truth. Nevertheless, or perhaps precisely because of this, the story was a complete success and inspired some years later Ernst Decsey and Gustav Holm to stage the comedy »Sissy's Brautfahrt«, which in turn was used by Ernst and Hubert Marischka as the basis for their musical comedy »Sissy«, first performed in1932. Around two years later, Marischka makes the film in which the young Romy Schneider plays herself into the hearts of millions as the delightful »Sissi«.

»The young Empress«, Pen drawing for an Elisabeth novel in »Kleinen Volksblatt«, 25th September 1933.

Film poster for the second part of Ernst Marischka's »Sissi« trilogy.

Opposite page:
Top: Scene from »Sissi«.
Middle: Scene from »Sissi – destiny years of an empress«.
Bottom: Scene from »Elisabeth of Austria« by Adolf Trotz with Lil Dagover as Elisabeth; 1931.

ELISABETH AND THE CINEMA

In the earlier films of the 1920s and 1930s, Elisabeth only played »supporting roles« in films about Emperor Franz Joseph or crown prince Rudolf and was hence depicted not as the young and charming Emperor's wife, but rather as a mature woman. It was not until Ernst Marischka's »Sissi« trilogy about the Austrian empress in the 1950s that Elisabeth became well-known and revered worldwide as »Sissi«. It was above all the young Romy

Schneider who contributed and who, still today, moulds the image of a young, sweet, easy-going »Sissi« albeit with little in common with the real empress Elisabeth. Characteristically, the end of the third part of the Sissi films coincides exactly with the time when Elisabeth breaks free from her role as empress and wife and forges an independent life according to her own ideas. This part of her life would not have fitted into the image of the loving wife, devoted mother and benevolent empress worried about the welfare of her people

SISSI, Schicksalsjahre einer Kaiserin

and winning their hearts, and was therefore left out at short notice. It was these circumstances which contributed primarily to establishing worldwide the romantic love story and the image of a popular empress and it is still thought today by many that Elisabeth died young since nobody knows anything about her later life.

Romy Schneider makes one more film appearance as empress Elisabeth: In his »Ludwig II.«, Luchino Visconti presents a capricious, disassociated Elisabeth, now worlds apart from the adorable Sissi from the 1950s. In this 1972 film, however, it is Elisabeth's cousin Ludwig who takes centre stage, showing nothing more than just a

snapshot of the empress.

So let's find out more about this historic Elisabeth!

THE BEGINNING

Above: The arrival of
the royal couple in Linz
an der Donau;
lithography by
Josef Edelbacher, 1854.

Opposite page:
Elisabeth at the age of
fifteen; photograph by
Alois Löcher, 1852/53.

Adolescence in Bavaria

Elisabeth is born on December 24th 1837 in Munich as the daughter of Duke Maximilian in Bavaria and Ludovika, the daughter of the King of Bavaria. Sisi, as Elisabeth is called by her family, is similar to her father in many respects: the duke loves the outdoor life and is a keen rider and traveller. Sisi enjoys a carefree childhood in Munich and at the family country estate of Possenhofen on Lake Starnberg, far removed from etiquette, ceremony and courtly constraints. In particular she liked the summer months in »Possi«, as the family calls Possenhofen, climbing, swimming and larking around with her brothers and sisters, Ludwig, Helene (»Néné«), Carl Theodor (»Gackel«), Marie, Mathilde (»Spatz«), Sophie and Max Emmanuel (»Mapperl«). This frolicsome and unchecked private life is only made possible because the Wittelsbacher line to which her father belongs has no official function at the Munich court. Her parent's marriage is not a happy one because they have little in common and their temperaments are so different. Ludovica devotes herself to her children and Sisi is to have a close, lifelong relationship to her mother, brothers and sisters. Duke Max does not think a great deal of family life and spends a lot of time with his mistresses and the illegitimate children. Sisi's first true love, at the age of 15, is Count Richard S, currently in the services of a duke and hence out of the question. He is sent away with an assignment at short notice, falls ill and dies shortly afterwards. Sisi is inconsolable and writes her first melancholic love poems.

Above: Duchess Ludovika in Bavaria; water colour by Bodo Winsel, 1848.

Middle: Duke Max in Bavaria, around 1850.

Below: Elisabeth's child glove.

Opposite page:
Top: Possenhofen country estate on Lake Starnberg, 1854.

Bottom: Sisi as an eleven-year-old with her favourite brother, Carl Theodor (Gackl), 1849.

THE BEGINNING

ENGAGEMENT IN ISCHL

In the summer of 1853, Sisi accompanies her mother and older sister Helene, called Néné, to Bad Ischl, to celebrate the 23rd birthday of her cousin, the young emperor Franz Joseph. The real reason for this journey, however, are marriage plans which are being hatched by the two mothers of Franz Joseph and Helene, who are

sisters. Franz Joseph is to become engaged to Néné. That is how the mothers planned it anyway, but it all turns out quite differently. The princess can not get changed on her arrival in Ischl because her luggage has not arrived. Néné is nervous and tense – there is a lot at stake for her. Whereas Sisi is carefree, naïve and being her usual self.

Above: Bad Ischl around 1850.

Below: Bone china rose bouquet, gift of reconciliation from emperor Franz Josephs to his bride; the reason is sadly not known.

It is love at first sight for Franz Joseph on seeing Sisi and dotes on: *Oh, but how sweet Sisi is, she's as fresh as a budding almond, and what a magnificent crown of hair frames her face! What lovely, soft eyes she has, and lips like straw-berries!*

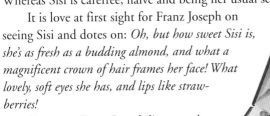

For once, Franz Joseph listens only to his heart and picks Elisabeth. The very next day Franz Joseph asks for her hand in marriage. When Sisi is asked, she bursts into tears: *How can he think of me? I'm so insignificant! – I am so fond of the emperor! If only he were not the emperor!*

The formal betrothal takes place on 19th August. Sisi is quiet, overawed by all the attention being paid her; Franz Joseph is overjoyed. His mother, Archduchess Sophie, takes pity on the frightened Sisi – after all she has

Opposite page: Elisabeth as bride; she is holding a miniature portrait of emperor Franz Joseph in her hand.

Elisabeth's trousseau list. Elisabeth's trousseau comprised of jewellery, gold accessories, gems, silver and wardrobe and was extremely modest for an empress-to-be.

nothing against her son's choice (as popular legend has it). Quite the opposite in fact – at the first public appearance at a ball to celebrate Franz Joseph's birthday she describes Sisi as *so charming, so humble, so blameless, so gracious …*, and romanticises about Sisi as a *Rose bud, opening up under the rays of the sun* and is especially pleased to see her son so happy.

After the betrothal in Ischl, Sisi returns to Bavaria, where preparations for the wedding begin immediately. Among other things, Sisi is prepared for her future role as empress of Austria - Sisi's unease and fear of the Viennese court grows. She feels that with her betrothal in Ischl she has set foot on the stage of world history, relinquishing her personal freedom.

Elisabeth in ivy leaf jewellery; Amanda Bergstedt from Franz Schrotzberg.

»OH MY LORD, WHAT A BEAUTEOUS DREAM«

Left: What is thought to be empress Elisabeth's ball gown; copy in the Sisi Museum from the original housed in the Museum of Fine Art, Vienna.

Below: The dress's stole with embroidered sultan's seal and Ottoman inscription.

O nly a few of Elisabeth's dresses have been preserved. One of these rare dresses is the ball gown which Elisabeth is thought to have worn at the farewell ball given on the

20th April 1854 just before her departure for Vienna. The original is held in the Historical Art Museum in Vienna but can no longer be displayed for conservation reasons.

A copy of the remarkable gown was made to commemorate the opening in April 2004 of the Sisi Museum in the Imperial Apartments in the Viennese imperial palace. It can be viewed exclusively in the Sisi Museum. During the course of the investigations for the reconstruction, it was the oriental decoration on the gown and

Departure of Elisabeth from Munich on 20th April 1854; lithography by Anton Ziegler.

the stole from the Institute Of Arabic Studies at the University of Vienna which were examined most carefully. It was established that the embroidery was not some fanciful decoration, but rather a »tugra« along with an ancient sultan's seal and an Ottoman inscription, the translation of which reads »Oh my Lord, what a beauteous dream«. Since no sources exist as to the origins of the robe, it can not be determined when, where and under what circumstances the robe was made. One possibility is that Elisabeth's father, Duke Max in Bavaria, who went on lengthy journeys, absorbed himself intensively with the Orient and published a book about his »Trips to the Orient« in 1839, had this unusual material made for the special occasion or perhaps had brought it back from a trip himself. Ehrenkleider, or uniforms of honour, were certainly typical marriage gifts in the Ottoman region. The inscription need not necessarily be related at all to the occasion of the forthcoming

wedding. The Sultan's seal as decoration and similar inscriptions on artefacts such as serving platters and candlestick holders are well-known in Ottoman culture.

Arrival of Elisabeth in Nußdorf bei Wien on 22nd April 1854; lithography by Vinzenz Katzler.

Below: Marriage contract from 4th March 1854.

THE WEDDING IN VIENNA

It was not a dream wedding. – Elisabeth becomes quieter in the days running up to the wedding. After the tearful farewell from her Bavarian homeland she travels with her parents from Straubing downstream to Vienna on the Danube, arriving on 22nd April. She had been prepared for the court ceremonial, but when Elisabeth pulls up in Vienna from Schönbrunn on 23th April in a grandiose stage coach pulled by eight Lipizzaner horses, it is not a radiant and beautiful bride for the emperor the cheering Viennese see but rather an exhausted, timid and sobbing

Right: Marriage
announcement of
the royal couple.

Below: The marriage
ceremony in the church
of St Augustin on
the evening of
24th April 1854;
anonymous lithography.

Opposite page: The royal
household is introduced
to the new empress.

young girl. She calms down a little on arriving at the imperial palace, where she is received ceremoniously by the emperor's family gathered there. Sophie noted in her diary that *Sisi was charming* and that *the conduct of the dear child was perfect, with sweet and graceful dignity.*

The wedding ceremony takes place on the 24th April 1854 in the church of St Augustin, the church of the imperial palace. The church of St. Augustin is decorated festively and illumi-

nated by 15,000 candles. The monarchy shows its splendid side. The ceremony is held by Archbishop Cardinal Rauscher of Vienna, accompanied by more than seventy bishops and abbots.

With all eyes fixed on her and the huge weight of expectancy, Elisabeth is overtaxed by the ceremonial celebrations. During her first reception as the new empress in the she bursts into tears of exhaustion and leaves the hall.

Elisabeth's wedding jewellery

Because there are no official accounts of the bride or the bridal couple, there has only been speculation so far about Elisabeth's wedding dress and her jewellery. In the course of researching for the new Sisi Museum, empress Elisabeth's original wedding jewellery was discovered in the treasure chamber in the Altötting pilgrim chapel in Bavaria. This place of pilgrimage for the Wittelsbach dynasty holds numerous valuable consecration gifts. The items in questions are a simple blossom crown made from golden web as hair decoration, a breast clasp and two combs inserted into the hair behind the ear, doubling up as ear decoration. Elisabeth the bride was therefore not adorned with precious jewellery but rather wore a plain, filigree blossom crown, in accordance with both the traditions of the conservative catholic House of Habsburg and the persona of a young and charming royal wife. The administrative chapel annals in Altötting record that the empress's

Above: The young royal couple, lithography by Eduard Kaiser, 1856.

Right: Empress Elisabeth's wedding jewellery; today it is kept in the treasure chamber of the Altötting pilgrims chapel in Bavaria.

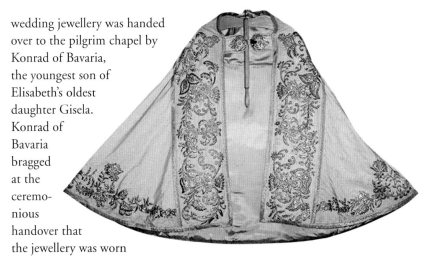

wedding jewellery was handed over to the pilgrim chapel by Konrad of Bavaria, the youngest son of Elisabeth's oldest daughter Gisela. Konrad of Bavaria bragged at the ceremonious handover that the jewellery was worn by his grandmother Elisabeth at her wedding, as well as a second time by his mother Gisela at her wedding to Leopold of Bavaria.

A honeymoon was out of the question due to the political situation – the Crimean War was raging. Officially the young royal couple spends their honeymoon at Castle Laxenburg near Vienna – however Franz Joseph rises early every day to attend to governmental matters at the imperial palace or Schönbrunn, not returning until late evening. Sisi is lonely and is homesick. Just a few days after her wedding – on May 8th, 1854 – she writes:

Pluvial with the silver embroidery of empress Elisabeth's wedding dress (see detail below), Moiré with silver embroidery. The empress's wedding dress was donated to the pilgrim basilica in Maria Taferl. Its embroidery was removed and transferred to the vesper robe, exhibited in the treasure room of the pilgrim basilica.

Oh, had I but never left the path,
That would have led me to freedom.
Oh that on the broad avenues
Of vanity I had never strayed!

POMP AND CIRCUMSTANCE

Above: Empress Elisabeth and emperor Franz Joseph (left and right on horses) with the French royal couple Napoleon III (standing on the left) and Eugenie (middle) in Salzburg; photograph from around 1867.

Opposite page: Empress Elisabeth (in the carriage) and emperor Franz Joseph (on horse) with crown prince Rudolf and his wife Stephanie in Laxenburg; painting by Karl Schwendinger, 1867.

Franz Joseph and
Elisabeth in front of the
Gloriette in the grounds
of Schönbrunn palace,
Ignatz Lechleitner
around 1854/1855

At the Viennese Court

From the very first day Elisabeth feels ill at ease in her new role, but initially tries to fulfil expectations. But from the very first day she finds her duties as empress awkward. She finds the pomp and court ceremonial tedious and despises the rigid hierarchical structures and intrigue at the Viennese court.

Sighing before the tired head
I remove the crown;
How many good hours has
the ceremony robbed me of today!

Court ball, 1887

As is so with ceremonial protocol and her position as first lady, she is continually surrounded by court ladies and ladies of the aristocracy who, she feels, are spying and watching her. On ceremonial occasions she feels according to her own words as if she is being paraded *like a horse in harness*. Sisi increasingly suffers from the loss of her personal freedom:

The young empress begins to suffer from sleeplessness, lack of appetite and a persistent cough. As a preventative measure against lung disease her doctors recommend that she is sent to Madeira. For the first time Sisi is again free of any obligation and enjoys life far removed from the constraints of the court. She prolongs her stay for treatment and tries to stay away from

I have awakened in a dungeon
With chains on my hands
And my longing ever stronger
And Freedom! You, turned from me!

8. Mai 1854

Vienna for as long as possible. She travels to Corfu and Venice and then on to Reichenau an der Rax and Possenhofen, staying well away from Vienna. When Elisabeth returns to the Viennese court after an absence of two years a profound transformation has taken place. The once graceful but shy and melancholic young girl has become a self-confident, proud beauty. It is in this period that the famous portraits by Franz Xaver Winterhalter are painted. The most famous one without doubt is from 1865 showing Elisabeth wearing a ball gown and diamond stars in her hair.

Above: Empress Elisabeth's original diamond star from the design by previous court jewellers Rozet & Fischmeister, Kohlmarkt 11. Elisabeth did not own just one set of 27 diamond stars, two versions of the splendid stars are in existence today. One version originates from the court jeweller Jakob Heinrich Köchert and is worked with a pearl in the centre, a second version without a pearl was made from a design by court jewellers Rozet & Fischmeister. Some stars were given to the ladies-of-waiting and are now in the possession of descendants, one set of 27 diamond stars was bequeathed within the family. These stars are depicted on a photograph, which shows the trousseau of archduchess Elisabeth (named Erzsi), the daughter of crown prince Rudolf, at her wedding to Otto Fürst Windisch-Graetz in 1902.

That Elisabeth also had a very sharp tongue is evident from her poetry, in which she writes of how unhappy she feels at the court and of her repugnance at the Vienna court establishment. In these poems she attacks the blatant hypocrisy, falseness and arrogance and openly settles scores with the imperial family:

The young royal couple in Venice, Anton Einsle 1856.

But my body, it is resting;
for my much-plagued spirit
is burdened now even more
And being fed on Viennese gossip.

The most noble names
of our aristocracy are coming
Medals of recognition – and palace ladies;
(they are mostly fat and stupid).

Oh, I know your behaviour!
Oh how much you have vilified me
Ever since my younger years
distorting your piousness.

Yes, you are great
at throwing stones at others!
under a phoney halo
You feel comfortable under it …

Court ball, 1887

Below: Detail of empress Elisabeth's black lacy stole, which she is wearing on the portrayal by Anton Einsle.

To Titania, adorn yourself
Today with diamonds!
It is Sunday and
the relatives are coming again …

The first to appear tends to be
Ob'rons youngest brother;
(and there is no such second
blighter on this planet).

In the sickly limp body
an apish being rules;
lying is his pastime
and also his duty.

Slander is his profession
This is what he has chosen;
That is why whoever crosses
       his path
he is lost already!

Now the flock of
all the wet-nurses and aunts,
Not having much spirit,
Inflated with pride.

This one is just as fat
as a Swiss cow,
proudly thinking quietly so high of herself
Right down to her stomach.

The other one as ugly as
a witch in a fairy-tale,
never having a good word
for anybody .

The other one there in gaudy peacock splendour
and false hair,
Oh, how she laughs sarcastically,
with her leaning head! …

Family dinner, 1887

Elisabeth is less and less in Vienna, spends a fortune on her expensive pleasures like riding and travelling and hardly takes part in public functions at the house of the emperor. The public become increasingly angered by her demonstrative indifference. The grand opening of the Vienna opera house, for example, is delayed specially for her at short notice because she stayed longer in Hungary than expected. She still does not attend the opening because she does not feel well. The empress's scarce presence gradually attracts innuendos in court circles, but Franz Joseph sticks to his wife and Elisabeth does not care at all about public opinion. Their silver anniversary in 1879 presents a suitable opportunity to counteract this bad image. On this occasion, Franz Joseph asked his wife to stand by him and, for his sake, she agrees to his request.

Reconstruction of empress Elisabeth's ruby jewel.
The crown jewels, including the ruby jewel, have been missing since 1918.
With funding from Sworovski, some selected pieces from the empress's
jewellery collection were reconstructed for the Sisi Museum using original
Swarovski crystals and in accordance with paintings and historical descriptions.
The items in question are Elisabeth's Hungarian
coronation jewellery, a set of her famous diamond
stars as well as ruby jewellery comprising of tiara, necklet and corsage,
reworked for Elisabeth in 1854. The magnificent ruby jewel, which Elisabeth
is wearing on the painting by Georg Raab, was originally Maria Theresia's
wedding present to her daughter Marie-Antoinette on her marriage in 1770 to
the French heir apparent and later King Ludwig XVI. Some years later in 1801 (other
sources mention 1787), the jewellery returns once again to the treasury in Vienna.
On 1st November 1918 the jewellery was taken from showcase XIII of the treasury
along with countless other jewellery items and jewels belonging to Leopold
Graf Berchtold, the chief treasurer emperor Karl I. They were taken to
Switzerland on 4th November. In 1919 the Swiss jeweller Alphonse de Sondheimer
(ennobled by Karl in 1921) was contacted with the intention of selling
the jewellery. In his memoirs Sondheimer describes the jewellery in detail and brags
that the stones were broken up and sold individually after it was deemed
the sale of the jewellery as a collection unfeasible. The Habsburg family
contradicts this version to this day and declares that the jewellery
in question had been stolen in exile.

The event is staged with much pomp. Her appearance at
the festivities causes a sensation, she is radiant, beautiful,
graceful and charming. Together with the emperor she
manages to get through the entire schedule, including the
acceptance of the homages from representatives from the
Crown lands, diplomats and European regents and the
receptions – lasting almost uninterrupted for three days.
Above all it is the accepting of congratulations from the
ambassadors of the Austrian Crown lands which is
strenuous: Standing around for hours, repeating the
same thank-yous time and time again. The newspapers
positively report that Elisabeth is present and that she
only occasionally rests for a few minutes at a time in a
chair placed especially for her in a reveal. The highlight is
the soirée in the imperial palace, which the 5,000 invited
guests attend: *At 9.45 the emperor appeared with the
empress on his arm … The arrival of the court was the*

Opposite page: Elisabeth
with ruby jewellery,
Georg Raab 1879.
The painting was for the
silver wedding of the royal
couple and is the last
portrait of the empress
for which she sat.

signal for those in the neighbouring rooms to leave and to assemble in the Knights Hall. Wearing his marshal uniform, the emperor led the empress to the middle of the hall. The empress continued to entertain while the emperor paraded up the hall, followed by archdukes and court knights. The empress's outfit was charming. The monarch wore a pearl-grey, high atlas dress with a white gauze plaid and long train. Rich embroidery adorns the robe. The train displayed elaborately stitched palm leaves. The diamonds and rubies on the vest sparkle like fire. The empress wore the same stones in her belt and in her necklet, comprised of three rows of diamonds and rubies. The tiara also had alternating large diamonds and rubies.

For Joseph's sake, Elisabeth made herself available for these pompous ceremonies. It was to be her last grand appearance.

Erzsébet királyné
Queen Elisabeth of Hungary

Elisabeth uses the power of her beauty quite deliberately to achieve her own ends. She has in fact little interest in active politics and interferes in her husband's affairs of government only once, to support the Hungarian cause. Elisabeth feels a great affection for the proud and temperamental Hungarian people, who have been under absolutist rule since the suppression of the revolution in 1849. Her favourite lady-in-waiting during the first few years, Caroline »Lilly« Hunyady is the first to talk passionately about her Hungarian homeland, Elisabeth starts to learn Hungarian in 1863 and in 1864 she sends for a young girl to the Vienna court as a reader – totally against the traditions of the court as she has no aristocratic parentage: Ida Ferenczy, who was to become her closest

Below left: Elisabeth as Queen of Hungary; Georg Raab, 1867.

Below: Empress Elisabeth's diamond crown. This lily crown, studded with diamonds and pearls and with a raised cross, was worn by Elisabeth at her coronation in 1867. It was similarly taken from the treasury by emperor Karl in 1918 and has been missing since. A large share of the diamonds can be traced back to one of Maria Theresia's house crowns and was worn, re-worked, by her successors.

Oh Hungary, beloved land of Hungary!
I know thee to be in heavy chains.
How I would like to offer my hand,
To rescue you from slavery!
Oh how I could give you the king!, 1886

Elisabeth as Queen of Hungary, historical photograph by Emil Rabending, 1866. The set of photographs of the empress was taken several months before the official crowning ceremony.

confidant and best friend. Ida is also a confidant of the Hungarian liberals Gyula Andrássy and Franz Deák and presumably initiated the first contact between Elisabeth and both politicians. Elisabeth becomes a fervent champion of Hungarian interests and has close contact with leading representatives of Hungarian. It is without doubt due chiefly to her efforts that Franz Joseph eventually signs the Compromise in 1866 recognising Hungary's historical rights and establishing the Austro-Hungarian monarchy. Finally, in 1867, the coronation of Franz Joseph, as well as that of Elisabeth to the Queen of Hungary, take place in the Cathedral of St Matthew in Budapest.

Elisabeth is crowned Queen of Hungary on 8th June 1867 in the Matthias church by placing the holy St. Stephans crown on her right shoulder. On her head she is wearing the house crown with diamonds which is shown on page 47.

FAMILY LIFE

Elisabeth and Franz Joseph's first daughter, Sophie, is born in 1855. Gisela is born in 1856. It was difficult to avoid initial differences of opinion with her mother-in-law, archduchess Sophie, as to how to bring up the children. Elisabeth wants to have her children around her, not in a »children's room« a long way from her apartment under the influence of her mother-in-law. She wants to take the children with her on journeys, whereas Sophie explicitly states that the journeys are too exhausting and dangerous for children. Archduchess Sophie does not try to take the children away out of hardheartedness; for her the welfare of the House of Habsburg is paramount and she believes that the empress's place is at her husband's side, whereby she does not have time to look after the children. Elisabeth insists on having the children around and makes Franz Joseph write

Elisabeth as young mother, water colour by Joseph Kriehuber, 1858.

the following letter to his mother: ... *After careful deliberation and after speaking to Sisi about it again, I am completely convinced that it is best for the children if they come into the Radetzky room ...Dear mum, you have guessed immediately as to why we want to do this move. I still implore you to judge Sisi leniently, if she is perhaps too jealous a mother, – she is after all such a devoted wife and mother! If you have the grace to quietly ponder the situation you will perhaps understand our distress at seeing our children shut up in your*

»The highest royal family«, photograph by Ludwig Angerer 1859. Characteristically there is only one single photograph showing Elisabeth together with her family and children. Depicted are Elisabeth sitting with Rudolf on her lap, Gisela, Archduchess Sophie and Archduke Franz Karl. Standing at the back, from left to right, are Franz Joseph, Ferdinand Max (later to be emperor of Mexico), his wife Charlotte, Franz Joseph's youngest brother Ludwig Viktor and Karl Ludwig. In contrast to Franz Joseph, Elisabeth does not once allow herself to be photographed with the children, not even with just one of them. Portrayals of the royal family are mostly photomontages so as to convey an impression of »normal« family life to the public (see also page 52).

apartment with shared anteroom, while poor Sisi has to struggle up the staircase only to find the children are hardly on their own, indeed to see strangers there, to whom you graciously show the children, shortening the few moments that I have time to be with the children.

Sophie backs down and the children move. But in 1857 the big shock came. Elisabeth had got her own way with her mother-in-law and takes her daughters on a journey to Hungary. Both daughters fall ill with diarrhoea and high temperature. Whereas Gisela recovers, Sophie dies at the age of two. Elisabeth is distraught, blames herself and, completely demoralised, finally gives up the initial conflict with her mother-in-law and the bringing up of her children. As much as Elisabeth feels close to her brother and sisters, she is alienated from her own children. During her lifetime, she is not to have a heartfelt relationship to Gisela or Rudolf, whose upbringing is assumed now by their grandmother. The only exception is her youngest daughter Marie Valerie.

CROWN PRINCE RUDOLF

The relationship between Elisabeth and her only son, crown prince Rudolf born in 1858, is extremely ambivalent. It is obvious to emperor Franz Joseph that his son and successor must continue the military tradition and appoints Rudolf patron of the 19th infantry regiment one day after his birthday on 21st August 1858. So Rudolf's path is mapped out by his father from birth, at the age of two Rudolf wears his first uniform; at the age of three and a half he has to accompany his father on hourly-long parading of the troops. To harden up and prepare the »wretch«, as Franz Joseph

Crown prince Rudolf; photograph by Josef Albert, around 1873.

called his sensitive son, for his military carrier, a strictly military upbringing was prescribed, turning him into a scared, nervous and sickly child and having a dramatic impact on his later life. His educator, Count Gondrecourt, prescribed draconian measures such as coldwater therapy, hourly-long exercising (of a seven year old!) in the cold and rain, nightly waking by shooting a pistol and the like and without any sense of pedagogic values whatsoever. During the first few years of Rudolf's life, Elisabeth is travelling most of the time and has only contact to her two children by letter during this period.

My dear Rudolf,

I have heard that you were very cross that I haven't written to you too. I thought you were too young to understand, but you too are sensible enough now, I will bring you back lots of nice toys. Can you remember me a bit? Heartfelt kisses from the bottom of my heart, my dearest boy your mum.

Letter from Madeira in 1861.

Above: Archduchess Gisela und Crown prince Rudolf in Venice; photograph by Julie and Fritz Vogel, 1861/62.

Opposite page: Family portrait on the occasion of the engagement of archduchess Gisela and duke Leopold of Bavaria (standing on the right); coloured photograph from a water colour by Emil von Hartitzsch (see also caption on page 50).

When Elisabeth does see Rudolf again in 1865 after a long period away, she finds him scared and nervous – to such an extent that she considers it *life-endangering*, believing that Gondrecourt's methods of upbringing must be turning Rudolf into a *halfwit*. She gives Franz Joseph an ultimatum: *It is my wish to reserve the unlimited rights in all aspects regarding the children, the choice of*

The official engagement picture of crown prince Rudolf and princess Stephanie of Belgium; Geruzet Frères studio, Bruxelles, 1880.

their environment, where they stay, control of their upbringing , in other words , it is my decision alone, until they come of age. Elisabeth. Ischl, 24th August 1865.

Franz Joseph backs down and Elisabeth consequently appoints Count Latour as Rudolf's educator. With a great deal of empathy, he accompanies the crown prince to the completion of his studies in 1877, becomes a sort of surrogate father and remains friends with him for the rest of his life. Latour ensures Rudolf receives a liberal, middle-class education, turning him into an open-minded and interesting man who despises the aristocratic lifestyle. His private circles are made up primarily of liberal intellectuals and academics, for which he is vehemently attacked by the conservative and clericalist Viennese court and why he makes adversaries of politically influential circles. Rudolf's political views stand in direct contrast to official court politics, forcing him into a life of secrecy. He encodes his political correspondence with encrypters and publishes his political articles anonymously. Rudolf leads for years a struggle for a challenge to suit his capabilities, but is ignored by his father his whole life. His private life is just as unsatisfying as his professional. Their daughter Elisabeth, Erzsi, is born two years after marrying Stephanie of Belgium in 1881. The marriage is initially harmonious and zealous, but over the years is threatened by their different personal agendas and

Crown princess Stephanie with her daughter Elisabeth; photograph by Othmar Türk, 1890.

the increased debauchery of the crown prince and finally fails as a result of a sexually transmitted disease Rudolf has and with which he infects his wife. Stephanie is from a staunchly catholic House, is haughty, loves pomp and ceremonial court life. Like his mother, Rudolf does not recognise snobbery and feels most comfortable in an informal atmosphere, preferable in the local inns. Because he had all but grown up without a mother, he has more of a heartfelt and intimate relationship to his governess and grandmother than he ever does to Elisabeth.

Rudolf condemns his mother's egoistic, eccentric and expensive lifestyle, she in turn can not cope with his secretive personality. Even her relationship with Stephanie is supposedly not a good one.

From 1888/89 Rudolf's state of mind as well as his health worsen dramatically. His failed struggle for recognition from his emperor father, his failed marriage , his incurable illness, countless love affairs, alcohol and

Above: Baronesse Mary von Vetsera; painting, around 1889.

Below: Crown prince Rudolf on his deathbed; 1889.

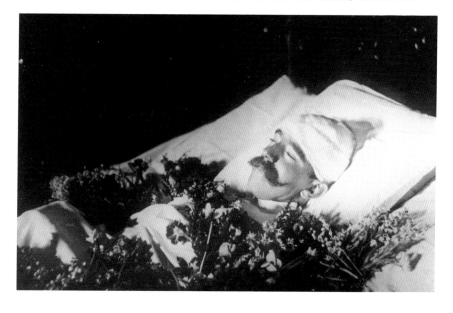

drugs had all made the 30-year-old Rudolf a desperate, resigned and broken man. He writes to his confidant Count Latour: *I see the inclined plane on which we slide downwards , understand what is going on but can not do anything, can't even speak loudly and say what I feel and think.*

On 30th January 1889 at the Mayerling hunting lodge, Rudolf shoots himself along with his last lover, 17-year-old baroness Mary Vetsera, who is prepared to die with him.

GISELA AND MARIE VALERIE

Elisabeth has an equally distant relationship with her eldest daughter as she has with Rudolf. Apart from that, Gisela is not a pretty girl and, in essence, takes after her father more than her mother. Gisela and Rudolf, who grow up together, are inseparable as children and have a close relationship with each other throughout their lives. In 1872 Gisela, aged sixteen, marries Prince Leopold of Bavaria, ten years her senior and second oldest son of the later prince regent Luitpold and Archduchess Auguste. The couple live in Munich and have four children. Elisabeth can not relate to Gisela's role as wife and loving mother. She always feels uncomfortable on familiar occasions, about the christening of her first grandchild, Gisela's daughter, she writes to Ida Ferenczy: *Thank God another day over. It is bitter for me to stay here, so lonely and without being able to speak to anybody. I miss you more than words can say. Today was the*

Archduchesses Gisela and Marie Valerie in Bad Ischl; photograph by Victor Angerer, 1871.

christening, mother and child are so healthy that they will go on to live to be 100 … With Gisela's second daughter, her distance to her grandchildren becomes even more apparent, as she writes to Rudolf: *The child of Gizela is unusually ugly, but amuses Valerie …*

The only exception in Elisabeth's relationship to her children is her youngest daughter Marie Valerie, born in the year after the coronation of the King of Hungary in 1868. She is the first child with which Elisabeth takes up the motherly role and wants to make up for what she missed with her older children. She always has Valerie with her, taking her on most of the journeys and positively showering her with her new-found motherly love, earning Valerie the name »The only child«. She organizes birthday parties for her and Valerie often has a guilty conscience that she is so obviously favoured over her brothers and sisters.

Above: Archduchess Gisela; photograph by Edlinger Ed., 1872.

Below: Archduchess Marie Valerie; photograph by Emil Rabending, 1872.

In 1890, and with her mother's backing, Marie Valerie enters into a love marriage with Archduke Franz Salvator from the Tuscany line. Elisabeth's relationship to her favourite daughter's children is, if anything, distant, because they always make her feel reminded of her age and own childhood. She

Archduchess Marie Valerie
and Archduke Franz
Salvator; photograph
by Adéle, 1890.

does visit more and more between trips, but usually
just stays a few hours, brings many presents and leaves
again straight away. Valerie notes in her diary: ... *Ella
was very close to her, mum enjoyed her company and messed
around with her more than I thought possible.*

The couple live predominantly in Wallsee Castle
in Upper Austria and have ten children. In 1919 she
signs the renunciation of estate and remains in Austria
retaining her assets.

THE FLIGHT

Above: Empress Elisabeth
and the widow of
Napoleon III, Eugenie,
on Cape Martin; photo-
graph from around 1895.

Opposite page:
Empress Elisabeth;
photograph by Ludwig
Angerer around 1860.

THE HORSEWOMAN

Riding has been one of Elisabeth's biggest passions since childhood. She had already learnt classical dressage from her father, now the empress trains intensively, distinguishing herself as one of the best and daring horsewomen in Europe. But she also wants to master the High School of Dressage and appoints the renowned dressage horsewomen Emilie Loiset and Elise Petzold from the famous Renz circus to learn tricks and show jumping. But she took most pleasure from wild hunt riding. After hunt riding in Hungary, where she has her own manege built in Gödöllő Castle in Budapest, she comes to England, spending many a light-hearted week

with her favourite pastime. John Welcome writes about Elisabeth's first riding stay in England: *She enjoyed those positions which accentuated her best qualities. She was cheerful and happy, and when she was happy she was gracious, considerate and noble – the exact opposite to the egoistic, introverted, moody creature at the Viennese court.*

One of the best riders in England, the Scottish Officer William George »Bay« Middleton is appointed to take on the captain and instruction responsibilities. Middleton is impressed by the pluckiness and perseverance of the empress and, with his help, she succeeds in becoming the only woman to reach the end of hunting races with, in some cases, up to a hundred riders and

Above: »Bay« Middleton guides Elisabeth during her riding stays in the years 1876 and 1878–1881; Basile Nightingale.

Opposite page: Empress Elisabeth on horse; steel engraving by Th. L. Alkinson, from around 1880.

where usually only a handful of them end the race. A hunt reporter writes: *We have never had such a bolder but still truly gracious parforce horsewoman!*

Further riding stays follow and Elisabeth, now with the help of Bay Middleton, begins to buy first-rate and extremely expensive horses for her private stables. Since she spends a lot of time with Middleton, rumours start about an alleged relationship between them and the gossip and intrigue ruins the stay in England for Elisabeth and it is prematurely cut short.

Above: Empress's leather riding fan.

Right: Under this photograph by Baader from the 1870s it states that *the empress is hiding from the photographer*.

At the end of the 1870s she hears that the most difficult and dangerous hunting rides takes place in Ireland. Elisabeth repeatedly spends several weeks at Lord Langford's Meath castle in Summerhill. Her parforce rides (extensive cross-country riding with jumping of obstacles such as hedges, walls or ditches) border on the impossible. Her lady-in-waiting, Marie Festetics, has grave concerns about the safety of the empress in these dangerous hunts which sometimes claim seriously injuries and writes in her diary: *The drops*

*are so high, the ditches and Doubles so deep
and also the Irish banks and walls and God knows
what else to break your hand, foot and neck. Never
do I hear so much about broken limbs as here and
every day I see somebody »carried«. Bayzand had
a bad fall, Middleton rolled over and even Lord
Langford, and so on. The empress has splendid
horses, Domino is the grandest, a magnificent black
horse, which to Lord Spencer's horror bolted off
at speed with Sisi on the first day. The field was
bordered by nasty fences, everybody's hair was on
end. What would she do? She had the presence of
mind to let the horse run, it successfully negotiated some
ditches and then she had him under control again
and galloped quietly back quietly … really, my hair often
stands on end.*

Above: Empress Elisabeth
on horse at the
Possenhofen country
estate; painting by
Carl Piloty, 1853.

Below: Empress
Elisabeth's saddle.

Elisabeth loves sporting challenges and is admired by
her companions for her courage and ability and is proud
to be the only woman (in the sidesaddle!) not to fail and
the only one never to have had a bad fall.

Here for the first time we encounter a side
of Elisabeth's personality that consciously seeks
out her own limits, among other things in
extreme sporting achievements where she
quite deliberately exposes herself to risk.

Elisabeth surprisingly gives up riding.
Rheumatism and sciatic nerve pains are
supposedly the reasons, but she tells her
lady-in-waiting Irma Sztáray later: *Suddenly
and without any reasoning I lost the courage and
I saw danger in every bush, danger I was scoffing
at only yesterday, and was not able to free myself from
this horror. This is the reason I never allowed Valerie
to mount a horse; I would never have been able to bear
the constant unease.*

Beauty cult

How beautiful she is! calls out the Shah of Persia against all etiquette when receiving Elisabeth in 1873.

Both men and woman of the time rave about the magical beauty of Elisabeth, but are allured even more by her grace, radiance and the mystical aura surrounding the empress.

Elisabeth is regarded as one of the most beautiful women of her time, something she is well aware off. Her beauty regime takes up a large portion of her daily schedule. Elisabeth is particularly proud of her thick, ankle-length hair, which is attended to between two and three hours every day. Her hairdresser Franziska (Fanny) Feifalik plays a decisive role here. The former hairdresser at the Vienna Burgtheater is responsible for the elaborate hairstyles and must always wear white gloves during hairdressing sessions, rings are not allowed. After the hourly-long hairdressing, plaiting and pinning-up, any resulting lost hairs must be produced in a silver dish, and every one results in a reproachable glance from the empress. Her niece Marie Larisch noted derisively, that *the hairs on Aunt Sisi's head are numbered.* The hair is washed every fourteen days with a specially prepared mixture made from egg yolk and Cognac, a procedure taking potentially up to a whole day. In later years she probably has her hair tinted with indigo and extract of nutshell. Elisabeth used the hairdressing sessions mainly to learn languages. Hungarian and, later, mostly old and new Greek. For the latter she appoints Constantin Christomanos, he reads out to her, corrects her exercises and philosophises with the empress. Constantin Christomanos, her reader, described these hairdressing sessions in the imperial palace as follows: *The hairdressing always takes almost two hours, she said, and while my hair is so very busy, my soul remains languid. I fear it is leaving through my hair into the fingers of the hairdresser. That is why my head hurts so much. The empress sat at a table, positioned in the middle of the room and covered with a white cloth. She is wrapped in a white peignoir decorated with lace, her hair let down to the floor and her physique completely enwrapped.*

To retain her much-admired beauty, Elisabeth tries out countless beauty formulae. She does not have her own secret recipe she swears by, but rather keeps on trying out new ones. The care products are prepared for her either in the court pharmacy or by a lady-in-waiting directly in her apartment. It is interesting that Elisabeth experiments less with fancy creams but rather attaches more importance to the different washing waters, tinctures and lotions which presumably produce better results. Elisabeth usually uses a simply toilet cream made up in the court pharmacy. This so-called Crème Céleste is made from white wax, ambergris, sweet almond oil

Above: Empress Elisabeth's hand mirror.

Opposite page: Elisabeth in the early morning light, copy by E. Riegele from the original by Franz Xaver Winterhalter, 1864. She only sat for a few painters, amongst them the portraits by Franz Xaver Winterhalter, Franz Schrotzberg and Georg Raab.

and rose water. Another cream, repeatedly ordered for Elisabeth (as shown by newly discovered beauty recipes) and highly regarded by the court ladies is the cold cream, made from sweet almond oil, cocoa

butter, bees wax and rose water. It owes its name to the cool refreshing effect the cream has on the skin: because the water-oil mixture is instable and breaks easily on the skin, the water dilutes quicker and the cream has a pleasant cooling sensation. In regard to facial waters, Elisabeth uses mainly rose facial water, to protect the skin against infections and impurities. The empress also tries out camomile roses, lavender and natural violet lotions. Elisabeth also swears by bizarre methods such as masks made from crushed strawberries or raw veal, with which she makes leather face masks and wears them overnight. In contrast to other women of her time Elisabeth disapproves of heavy make-up or perfume, keeping to more natural treatments and merely having her magnificent hair sprinkled with perfume essences. Elisabeth devotes considerably more time to treating her legs than her face. Elisabeth takes a bath daily, alternating between steam, oil and then back to cold baths. Elisabeth particular likes taking warm olive oil baths to retain delicate and supple skin. To conserve her slenderness, she often sleeps with cloths soaked in toilet vinegar above her hips. Her favourite vinegar is violet vinegar, made from freshly picked violet blossom, apple vinegar, distilled water and violet powder. *Place the violet blossom in layers in a bellied bottle and pour the*

Above: Empress Elisabeth's beauty recipes.

Below: Empress Elisabeth's perfume bottle.

Opposite page: Elisabeth in front of the evening sky; painting by Franz Xaver Winterhalter, 1864.

apple vinegar over it. Close tightly and let stand for two days. Then filter with a hair sieve and squeeze out the blossom with a wooden spoon. Remove some of the distilled water and mix the violet root powder in it. Pour into the distilled water and shake the mixture well.

Moreover, Elisabeth does not sleep with a pillow, arguably to preserve her upright posture and because she apparently wraps cloths around her neck, soaked in »Kummerfeldsch« ionised washing water. Her beauty cult becomes a lifelong challenge, assuming proportions which are commented critically on by her niece Marie Larisch: *She worshipped her beauty like a heathen his idols, going down on bended knee before it The sight of the perfection of her body was aesthetically pleasing to her; anything tarnishing this perfection was inartistic and unpleasant for her.*

Above: Empress Elisabeth with blue band; Franz Schrotzberg, 1862.

Below: The empress's toilet table in the Vienna Hofburg.

She feels her only flaw are her teeth, which she always tries to conceal by hardly opening her mouth

Empress Elisabeth's black bracelet. The simple filigree work originates from the time around 1880/1890 and shows an imitation gem portraying a »Bacchante«. Elisabeth is not a great wearer of jewellery and hardly wears any in private. It is only at the grand, prestigious occasions that she wears valuable jewellery. So as not to be distracted whilst riding she takes off all her rings, including her wedding ring, which she wears on a small chain around her neck. She never wears earrings either. The only jewellery she does wear are plain bracelets. She probably acquired this bracelet on one of her journeys and passed it on to a family member.

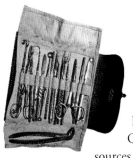

when she speaks, a habit which often makes conversation with her rather laborious. Elisabeth's bad teeth are not a result of a lack of hygiene, as often alleged. Quite the opposite in fact, new sources prove regular contact to her dentist. Elisabeth attaches great importance to teeth hygiene and regularly summons her dentist, Raimund Günther von Kronmyrth, a senior civil servant. Ironically, Rosa Albach Retty, Romy Schneider's grandmother, started the rumour that one afternoon she had seen a slim woman in the Zauner pastry shop in Bad Ischl, dressed in black and instantly recognisable as empress Elisabeth, surreptitiously cleaning her false teeth in a glass of water. Historic sources and facts categorically disprove this image. The empress's postmortem examination findings highlight the empress's good teeth *(bonne dentation)*, even the correspondence mentioned above between the empress and her dentist paints a completely different picture. Because Elisabeth places great importance on her perfect appearance and tries to conceal the smallest of imperfections as best she can, it is certainly conceivable that Elisabeth does not try to conceal her bad teeth but rather, in her view, her less than impeccable teeth(Even as a young girl she spoke quietly and unclearly, but this

Left: The dentistry hygiene set belonging to the empress's dentist.

Scales in the Vienna Hofburg.

was down to her shyness.) One explanation for Elisabeth not having pearl white teeth is that she smokes and has discoloured teeth possibly as a result of smoking filterless tobacco.

Elisabeth pays particular attention to her slim figure. She was 172 cm tall and weighed between 45 and 47 Kg. She has an incredible 51cm waistline, although we must keep in mind that women at that time wore tightly laced corsets which changed the natural body shape. She took exercise everyday to stay slim. In addition to riding she also enjoys fencing and swimming. For her daily exercise regime she has gymnastic apparatus installed in her toilet area in the imperial palace - wall bars, horizontal bars and rings attached between the doors. She trains here daily for one hour to stay fit and agile. In 1892 Constantin Christomanos wrote in his diary: *She called me into the salon today before going out. Mounted on the open door between the salon and her boudoir there were ropes, gymnastics and hanging apparatus. I met her just as she was lifting herself up with the hand rings. She was wearing a black silk dress with*

Menu from 9th June 1867
(Budapest)
Soup with small turkey dumplings
Fowl in aspic with Russian salad
Small »Palestine-style« vol-au-vents
»Emperor-style« topside beef
Semi- frozen pineapple punch
»Hunters-style« sautéed fillets of deer with puree
Natural green beans garnished with Villeroy calf's brain
Young, spit-roasted poulards
Mixed salad
»French-style« plum pudding
Mixed compote with plums from Bordeaux
Liptauer cheese
Iced strawberries and oranges
Fruit
Selection of breads

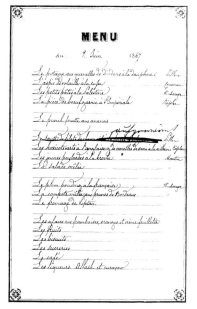

*a long train lined with magnificent
ostrich feathers. I had never seen her
dressed so grandiose. It was certainly
a picture to behold seeing her there
hanging on the ropes, a cross between
snake and bird. To get down she had
to jump away over a rope stretched just
above the floor. The rope is there so I
don't forget how to jump. My father
was a passionate hunter before God,
and he wanted us to learn to leap
like chamois ... if the archduchesses
knew that I have been exercising in
this dress they would run cold. But
I only did it en passant, normally doing it in the morning
or the evening.*

Above: Empress Elisabeth's
toilet and gymnasium
room in her apartment in
the Vienna Hofburg.

Below: Rare roasted lamb
filet with vegetables and
potatoes, arranged on
a serving dish from the
empress's cruise service.

After she is forced to give up riding at the beginning
of the 1880s due to severe attacks of rheumatism she
compensates with hours of rapid hiking in heat as well
as gales and rain. The tours lasted up to nine hours and
did not only severally test the court ladies, who had
already been put through physical endurance trials before
being employed. It was not uncommon even for local
guides to force a return after a few hours completely
exhausted on the basis of
»suddenly having no
knowledge of the area«.
Additionally Elisabeth
tries out different diets
to keep her weight.
Here the scales play a
decisive role: Elisabeth
weighs herself daily and
enters both her weight
and her daily exercise
schedule in a notebook.
As she gets older, she tries

Right: Invoice from the royal court suppliers Demel.

Below: Her Majesty's sour cherry cake by Demel, served on the »Elisabeth silver« bought for Elisabeth in 1852, Dessert plate from the royal »Hofform« service.

out more and more excessive diets. Amongst them are days without eating at all, days when she drinks only milk or eats only oranges or meat broth. However, the rumours that Elisabeth drinks raw meat juices are exaggerated. It is true that raw legs of veal are delivered daily to the empress but, after being cut into pieces and pressed with a duck press, an extract is boiled for Elisabeth to drink. Equally consigned to the realms of legend is that Elisabeth continually starves to stay slim. Receipts from different pastry shops show that Elisabeth is especially fond of confectionary and ices. Original menus also show that Elisabeth indeed has a very healthy appetite: her usual breakfast consists of coffee with cold and warm cream, sweet and savoury pastries, eggs, cold cuts, honey, fruit and various kinds of bread rolls. With a glass of wine.

Of particular importance to her are fresh milk and milk products. In 1895 she even establishes her own small dairy-farm in the palace grounds at Schönbrunn for the provision of daily supplies of fresh milk. On journeys – even at sea, she takes goats with her to have fresh milk daily. Not without a certain self-mockery she tells Christomanos, who accompanies her on many journeys, about one goat who travelled with them: *She comes on the journey without having an eye for beauty. But she has a sense of duty, for she is an English women ... There are no better nurses than English women.* Elisabeth has a particular weakness for French oysters, eating them at every opportunity on her journeys, accompanied by Asti spumante. One thing that can be guaranteed at dinner, consisting mostly of a roast withvegetables, is ice-cream desert, or rather sorbet, since it is not prepared with cream or milk. Elisabeth's favourite ice cream is violet flavour. This is prepared by pounding a handful of violet leaves in a mortar, adding some warm water and sugar and allowing the mixture to freeze after an hour.

Two factors have possibly contributed to the rumour mill surrounding the Empress's fanaticism for dieting. On the one hand, Elisabeth never attempted to emulate any popular beauty ideals. A »pretty« women at that time was considerably more rounder and fuller. It was photographs like that of Katharina Schratt, who later became Franz Joseph's companion or Mary Vetseras, crown prince Rudolf's lover who died with him, which really portray the then beauty ideal. It was on this basis that Elisabeth was considered slim by all around her, something which needs to be put into context in terms of what was perceived to be »lean« and »healthy« in those days. Her disposition could well have played a key role, her brothers and sisters are very slim and tall. On the other hand, Elisabeth had her own eating habits. She ate a generous breakfast, lunch, often a small snack and one small, final meal between 5pm and 6pm. She knows from experience that large meals late on do not agree with her or she puts on weight and so therefore does not want to eat anything after 6pm. It is for this reason that she tries to stay away from the usual evening family dinner as often as possible. Should it not be possible

Above: The empress's duck press.

Below: Menu from the wedding of archduchess Marie Valerie and archduke Franz Salvator on 31st July 1890 in Bad Ischl.

to avoid attending, she eats demonstratively little, contributing to the rumour mill that she does not eat anything.

BEAUTY ALBUM

Elisabeth's beauty cult is not limited to just herself – she is fascinated by every aspect of beauty and invests in a beauty album. She collects photographs of women she considers beautiful: Ladies-in-waiting, European rulers and also ladies from the demimonde such as dancers and circus artistes. Elisabeth is fascinated more by radiance and natural or unusual faces, not by beauty in its classic sense and, above all, irrespective of class or social parentage.

Left: Empress Eugénie. The empress of the French was regarded as somewhat of a European rival to Elisabeth in the beauty stakes. Count Wilczek recounts that he had casually watched both empresses at a meeting of the royal couple in Salzburg: *I opened the door very quietly and had to go through two empty rooms in the apartment, through the bedroom to the toilet closet, whose door was half open. Opposite was a large mirror and, with their backs turned to the door I was standing behind, were both empresses busily measuring surely the most beautiful fibulas in the whole of Europe with two centimetre measures. It was a sight to behold and I will never forget it for as long as I live.* Elisabeth's niece, Marie Larisch, disagrees with this rumour however, discounting it simply as name-dropping. As far as she could remember, they had never been on amicable terms.

From empress Elisabeth's beauty album:
clockwise from top left: Madame
Duz-Oglu from Constantinople,
Caroline »Lilly« Hunyady, Elisabeth's
lady-in-waiting, Mademoiselle Léonie
from Paris, variety artist and
an unknown dancer.

Opposite page: Empress Elisabeth at the window of the Albert studio in Munich, 1865.

Above left: Elisabeth as Queen of Hungary; Emil Rabending, 1866.

Above right: Elisabeth before 1860.

Below: Photograph by Emil Rabending, 1865/66.

The photographs on these double page are amongst the few authentic photographs of the empress. Most of the images of Elisabeth represent photomontages.

Hiking wear instead of Haute Couture

Elisabeth is certainly aware of her obligation as empress to dressing fashionably and considers it her duty to dress well although she does not think it important to dress in the latest fashion. Elisabeth places great importance on showing off her slim, elegant figure. Yet her clothing must be comfortable and allow for as much freedom of movement as possible. It is primarily riding clothes that play an important role. Elisabeth spends many hours

trying on clothes and is difficult to please. She has a saddled wooden horse erected in front of a large mirror specifically for this purpose to study the cut of the clothes and how they hang. Clothes were not only tailored directly on the body of the empress, she also had herself sewn into her clothes, a procedure which can take up to an hour. On journeys she likes wearing outfits made of hard-wearing woollen material with button-up skirts so they can by shortened so as not to hinder her when walking. It is for this reason that she does not wear petticoats but instead tight leg wear – made from silk tights for the summer and from fine doeskin for the winter. Her shoes are particularly conspicuous – as the »First Lady« she does not wear silken half-boots with heels, but rather comfortable, flat, leather shoes, mostly ankle-high laced boots which she can also use for the extended walks and hikes in all weathers.

Opposite page, top: The empress's cream coloured dress. The dress is thought to be from 1889 and was the only »bright« dress which Elisabeth wore after the suicide of her son. She wore it for special occasions such as the birthday of the emperor and the anniversary of the engagement of her daughter Marie Valerie.

Opposite page bottom: Empress's brown lace shawl.

Top: Elisabeth in a white dress, from around 1863.

Right: The empress's dressing gown.

Below: Glove with glove box, splendid Rococo style fans and the empress's embroidered slippers.

Posthumous portrait of the empress by Anton Kaulbach. He paints Elisabeth with the often quoted, white parasol lined with leather and the leather fan she never left home without.

FLEEING
THE STRANGE GLANCES

So as to be remembered as a young and beautiful woman, Elisabeth refuses to let herself be photographed from her early 30s, the last portraits of her to be painted from life were in 1879 when she was 42. Fans, veils and parasols become the empress's indispensable companions. She hates being gawped at and from then on conceals her face from the gaze of strangers.

Elisabeth was petrified of getting older, confiding in Marie Larisch: *O, how ghastly it is to get old! To feel the hand of time on our body, watching the skin wrinkle, waking in the morning dreading daylight and knowing that you are no longer desirable.*

These lines reveal that Elisabeth evidently values her self-esteem to a large degree in terms of her beauty. When she sees her beauty waning, she no longer considers herself desirable as a woman, she feels useless and falls into depression. Parasols and fans not only conceal her, at least in her opinion, vanishing beauty, but increasingly become symbolic barriers between herself and her environment. In 1892 her Greek reader Constantin Christomanos writes in his diary: *I again saw this parasol and fan – the renowned black fan and the universally known white parasol – faithful companions of her outer existence, which have almost become a component of her physical appearance. They are not, in her hand, what they signify to other women, but rather just emblems, weapons and shields serving her true self...she wants to repel only the outer life of people as such ...*

*If time ever touches me,
I will veil myself,
and the people will speak of me
as the woman, who once was.*

*It stirs my bile,
When they stare at me so,
I would like to creep into a shell
And could die of rage.*
                    To the starers, 1887

From the top down:
Empress's black
lacy umbrella,
black circular fan,
doubling up as a
sunshade, and one
of the empress's
black lacy fans.

»Lady in black«. Staging
by Rolf Langenfass in the
Sisi Museum, Vienna.

I wander lonely from this earth,
Long have I turned from joy, from life,
No companion shares the life of my soul.
There has never been a soul that understood me.

To the future-spirits, 1887

LADY IN BLACK

After the tragic suicide of her only son Rudolf in 1889 Elisabeth becomes increasingly bitter, withdrawing into herself more and more, becoming reclusive and unapproachable. She wears only black and most people now only experience Elisabeth as a black silhouette in the distance.

Above: The royal couple at the Hungarian millennium celebrations in Ofen castle on 8th June 1896.

Her last public appearance is at the millennium celebrations in Budapest in 1896. Kalman Mikszáth, who is present at the reception in Budapest castle, narrates his impressions: *There she sits in the throne room of the royal castle in her black Hungarian garment, embroidered with laced. Everything, everything about her is morbid. A black veil flows down from her black hair. Black hairpins,, black pearls, everything is black, only the visage as white as marble and unutterably sorrowful ... A Mater dolorosa ... She still is one, but the heartache has left its mark carved in this visage ... not a single movement, not a single glance revealing any interest. There are similarities to a pale-faced marble statue ...*

REFUGES

With time, Elisabeth learns to defend her interests at court and begins to lead a life that corresponds to her own ideas. She now does exactly what she wants and increasingly refuses to fulfil her official role as empress. Franz Joseph and Elisabeth become estranged: Elisabeth feels incapable of standing at his side and puts her own interests first. Elisabeth refuses to fulfil the traditional duties of wife, mother and empress imposed by the court, but does not seek any other fulfilling tasks in life – her lady-in-waiting Countess Festetic worries about this, writing: *She is a daydreamer, and her chief occupation is brooding.*

In order to distract herself Elisabeth goes on long journeys and seeks out refuges, places where she can live in freedom. These include the Hungarian chateau of Gödöllő near Budapest, the Hermesvilla in the Lainzer Tiergarten on the outskirts of Vienna as well as the Achilleion on the Greek island of Corfu.

Gödöllő castle, Budapest, Hungary. The former Grassalkovich castle was given to the royal couple by the Hungarian state in celebration of the coronation of the King of Hungary in 1867.

She feels particularly at ease in Hungary, even her closest and most private space with Ida Ferenczy, Marie Festetics and later with Irma Sztáray, is Hungarian. It is her favourite language and she speaks to her ladies-in-waiting only in Hungarian. Elisabeth visits Hungary regularly, especially Gödöllő where she has her privacy and feels at ease.

Corfu is an ideal place to stay, the climate, the walks in never-ending shade of the olive branches, good driveways and the glorious see air ... she writes to Franz Joseph in 1888 and regards this secluded place, with its delightful scenery, as her future home. She has a grand and extremely expensive Villa built in Pompeian style, furnishes it with valuable antiques and names it after her favourite hero, Achilleus, from Greek mythology. She calls it ... *my sanctuary, where I may belong to me* ... But just a short time later the restless empress even losses interest in the Achilleion, feeling burdened and cramped by it and she wants to put it up for sale. In the event, it remains unsold until after her death. The agonising sense of unease drives her forward. She is criticised more frequently behind closed doors for her extravagances and eccentricity, but Franz Joseph supports his wife, whom he loves more than anything, wherever he can, even if this means that he has

Hermes Villa in the Lainzer Tiergarten, Vienna. The Hermesvilla in the Lainzer Tiergarten, completed by Carl Hasenauer in 1883, was a present from Kaiser Franz Joseph to Elisabeth in the hope that it would bind the empress more to Vienna.

…my sanctuary, where I may belong to me…

Elisabeth about the Achilleion

to tolerate her absence from his side even more. They meet up several times a year and spend a few days together, the rest of the year Franz Joseph relies on letters from his wife with detailed accounts of her travels and constantly lives in fear for her.

Table service from the Achilleion. Irma Stáray continues: *Meals on the Achilleion were indeed splendid. For the splendid dishes we thank the sea, reminded to us by each piece of the dinner set, in as much as that the silver, porcelain, glass and linen items from the emperor crown displayed a dolphin. This was the style of the Achilleion, where the dolphin is prominent on just about every artifact and ornament.*

Below: Jewellery box from the Achilleion.

Opposite page, above:
Achilleion: Elisabeth's lady-in-waiting Irma Sztáray relates: *The peristyle is the silent witness to the lonely walks of the empress. Nobody disturbs her here, nobody dare come here without first being summoned …* She is particularly impressed by the evening light which is at its most beautiful at full-moon: *… it was not just the peristyle that swam in a sea of light, the arc lamps light down ominously on to the terraces, sweeping down from the garden. It was just as if I had entered a mystical world of fairy-tales …*

Opposite page, below:
Achilleion villa on Corfu, Greece. The architect of the villa, completed in 1891/92, was the Neapolitan Raffaele Carito.

Titania

I hasten into the land of dreams,
My master there are you,
My soul awaits you
enthusiastically!
To my master, 1887

Elisabeth, who has written poetry since her youth, uses lyrical poetry more and more as a means of escape. She loves Homer and writes numerous poems inspired by her great idol, Heinrich Heine, which reveal not only her disappointment, melancholy and longings but also her misanthropy and increasing isolation.

Above: The empress's poetical diary.

Below: Heinrich Heine; painting by Gottlieb Gassen.

Titania should not go among people
In this world, where no one understands her,
Where a hundred thousand gawpers surround her
Whispering inquisitively: »Look, the fool, look!«
Where ill will is wont to follow her enviously with his eyes,
Misrepresenting each of her actions,
She should return home to those spheres,
Where finer, more related souls do dwell.
To Titania, 1888

In his memoirs, Constantin Christomanos eternalises his memories of the reading hours with the empress, at which Heine was omnipresent: *Whilst discussing life and the way of the world, she began to declaim with a voice of fluent irony* ... followed by the 58th poem of the return cycle from the »Buch der Lieder« (»Book of Songs«). Elisabeth's adoration of the poet, who died in 1856, can also be interpreted as a sign of her spiritual independence and autonomy. At this time, Heine is far from being a recognised poet, but it is precisely his realism on contemporary issues and sense of irony, which sparks a European scandal, which appeals to her. It is also the very fact that he is considered an out-sider which makes him likable.

Elisabeth also begins to identify with the fairy queen Titania in Shakespeare's »Midsummer Night's Dream«. Franz Joseph can not fully under-

Above: Living room and bedroom of the empress in the imperial palace. She composed many of her poems at her writing table in the reveal

Left: The empress's writing set made from gilt silver and lapis lazuli.

stand his wife's fantasies, but as a treat, has her bedroom at the Hermesvilla in Vienna adorned with frescoes from Midsummer Night's Dream , calling it »Titania's magic castle«.

On her travels

Elisabeth's Wanderlust gets stronger – the further away she is from Vienna, the better she feels. Under the pretence of worsening health, the empress ventures on long journeys, wanting to get to know foreign countries and cultures. But not only that. Most of all she enjoys the easy-going life without obligations or restraints and being able to do as she pleases. She refuses to play the role of empress of Austria, but of course does enjoy taking advantage of the perks of the job, especially the financial ones. The hitherto unknown diary of her butler,

Eine Möwe bin ich von keinem Land,
Meine Heimath nenne ich keinen Strand,
Mich bindet nicht Ort und nicht Stelle,
Ich fliege von Welle zu Welle.

A seagull am I, from no land I come,
There is no beach that I will call home,
Bound by no destination or place;
Flying from wave to wave I race.

North Sea songs 7, 1880

Leopold Alram, tells of the carefree days on the Côte d'Azur mainly visiting pastry shops, shopping and calling on those yachts belonging to rich Americans or to the rich European aristocracy such as the Rothschilds: *On the 19th March travelled again to Nice with Her Majesty and countess Mikes* (Elisabeth's lady-in-waiting); *breakfast in Nice at Cafe Rumpelmayer Her Majesty and Lady Count, visit to the shops … Early on 30th March train journey with Her Majesty and the countess to Cannes, ate breakfast there at Cafe Rumpelmayer, then visit to the shops … During this outing I was given the noble honour of being allowed to take off the shoe of Her Majesty, the noble lady changed shoes, the countess could not manage*

Left: Empress Elisabeth on board a ship. The water colour was created by Leopoldine Ruckgaber from a photograph on the request of Marie Valerie.

Below: Leopold Alram's diary, 1893–1896 empress Elisabeth's butler.

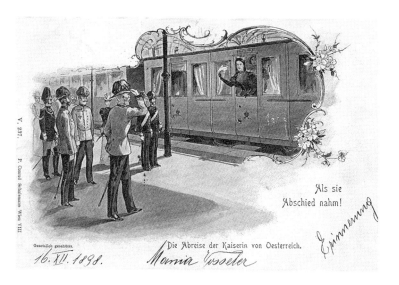

Gesetzlich geschützt.

Die Abreise der Kaiserin von Oesterreich.

Als sie Abschied nahm!

Erinnerung

16. XII. 1898.

Above: Elisabeth departing; commemorative postcard, 1898.

Below the salon of the imperial salon carriage; opposite, top the technical layout; opposite, bottom, the empress's sleeping compartment.

The empress's imperial salon carriage. Whilst Elisabeth is modest during her cruises, her specially built imperial salon carriage, built in 1873 and used to travel through the whole of Europe, is appointed luxuriously. The imperial salon carriage, comprising of one salon carriage and one sleeping carriage, is appointed with electric lighting, steam heating and a toilet for the empress. The original is in the Technical Museum Vienna and a true reproduction of the salon carriage is in the Sisi Museum.

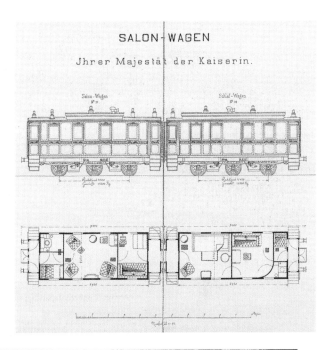

SALON-WAGEN

Jhrer Majestät der Kaiserin.

Salon-Wagen
N° 31.

Schlaf-Wagen
N° 32.

this task so they called in me, it went well because I am after all an expert in this regard. Upon successful completion Her Majesty asked of me whether I had often taken off ladies shoes, in

Above: On the deck of the yacht Miramar; empress Elisabeth in the background with the sunshade; photograph by archduke Franz Salvator, 1894.

Below: Empress Elisabeth's travel service; Mayerhofer & Klinkosch.

response to my negation she said: Then I am astonished that you managed to do it so well thank you very much indeed.

And a few days later: *Took the train at 9.30 from Menton to Nice with Her Majesty, Lady Countess Trany, Lady Countess Mikes and Ms Schmidt, viewed there the rich American Panterbil's* (presumably meaning the American Industrialist Frederick William Vanderbilt) *ship named Valiant lying at anchor in Nice harbour then the Rothschild's ship (Eros). Valiant is supposed to have cost 2 Million Florins a huge palace of a ship ... hereafter light refreshment at Cafe Rumpelmayer ...*

The longer the journeys continue, the higher are the Empress's spirits. She likes her glamour shared with the ordinary every now and again. During her hikes she likes stopping off for a bite to eat in ordinary alpine cabins or village inns to drink a glass of milk or have a

few pretzels with a glass of beer. It is essential that she remains unrecognised, as soon as she senses she is being stared at or has been recognized, she takes flight straight away.

Elisabeth does not travel the world aimlessly and haphazardly, as often portrayed. Quite the contrary, she plans her route down to the last detail a year in advance, only her closest confidants and attendants are let in on the plans and sworn to secrecy. Elisabeth usually adheres strictly to this itinerary, only prolonged bad weather occasionally forces her to change her plans. For all that, Elisabeth is constantly on the move, the thought of staying in one place for too long cramps her. To Constantin Christomanos she says: *The destinations are made desirable only by the travelling in-between. If, on arrival some-where, I knew that I would never leave, my stay in a paradise would be hell.*

Above and left: Dolphin handles from the dinner service for the yacht Miramar; silver-plated alpaca, Arthur Krupp, Berndorf 1893.

Below: The yacht Miramar.

A gift to the empress: A casket with four boards, making a relief map of the route from Vienna to Corfu when put together.

Elisabeth loves cruises most of all, finding the lure of the infinite ocean irresistible and dreams in her poems of soaring free like a seagull: Elisabeth does not suffer from seasickness and loves the swell when she can feel particularly close to the elements. On the deck of her yacht is a glass pavilion with unobstructed view of the sea. In stormy weather, with the entire crew fearing for their lives, she has herself tied to a chair, declaring to the surprised Christomanos: *I do this like Odysseus, because the waves lure me.*

The empress's companions are less keen on the forces of nature on the high sea. Elisabeth's butler Leopold Alram, who accompanies the empress on her sea voyages over many years from 1893, notes in his diary: *The sea was dreadful, our ship was tossed around like a nutshell, the tossing and turning was dreadful, we thought we'd be fish*

bait; at 9.30 in the evening we turned round, I
tied a serviette around my head so as not to hear
anything ...

Previously unpublished letters from Marie
Festetics indicate that the empress's journeys,
especially those at sea, were both physically and
mentally gruelling for her companions, and
also show Elisabeth's increasing egomania: *It is*
becoming increasingly unbearable on board ...
Her Majesty is occupying the entire ship. In the
evenings, or when it rains, there is nowhere to go. Her
Majesty recounts the most intimate things, she is very
endearing and means well, but I often cringe at the beauteous
spirit sinking into egoism and paradox.

Above: Medical kit from
the empress's luggage.

Below: The Rumpelmayer
pastry shop in Menton
on the Côte d'Azur.

On one journey in 1888, which she leads to Greece
and Small Asia, Elisabeth has an anchor tattooed on
her shoulder. Franz Joseph is appalled. Marie Valerie
finds out about this on the day of her engagement and
portrays the scene in her diary. Elisabeth has just given
her approval to Valerie's marriage and mother and
daughter burst out in tears of joy and emotion,

MENTON

... when Papa came in and asked me whether I had been crying about the dreadful shock of finding out about mum having had an anchor burnt into her shoulder, something I found very original and really not that shocking ...

LONGING FOR DEATH

Elisabeth's melancholy becomes increasingly stronger and appears temporarily to have completely taken over her. A distraught letter from her companion Marie Festetics to Ida Ferenczy (written at Corfu on November 11th 1888), for

Empress Elisabeth as an adult; Leopold Horovitz from around 1900, posthumous picture from a photograph by Ludwig Angerer 1868/69.

whom the gruelling journeys are too arduous and can no longer travel with Elisabeth, lead one to assume Elisabeth has deep depression: *Dear Ida, what I am seeing and hearing here saddens me. Her Majesty is indeed always endearing when we are together and talks as she once did. She is however no longer her old self – a shadow lies over her soul. I can only use this expression for a person who suppresses and negates all the beauty and nobility of feelings out of convenience or entertainment – it can only be bitterness or cynicism! Believe me that my heart is crying tears of blood. She does things to make your heart stand still and things which are beyond comprehension. We had bad weather yesterday morning, but she still set sail. It started to pour down at 9 in the morning, accompanied by thunder until*

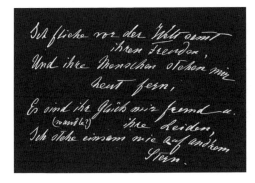

I flee from the world and its joys,
its people have become strange to me;
and also their happiness and sorrows;
I stand lonely, like on a star ...

To the future-spirits, 1887

3 in the afternoon. During the whole time she sailed around us, sitting on deck, holding the umbrella above her and was very wet. Then she alighted somewhere, called for her carriage and wanted to stay the night in a stranger's villa!

Thoughts of death take an increased hold of her from 1897. Irma Sztáray, her lady-in-waiting, travelling companion and closest confidant during this period noted in her diary: *Thoughts of death encircle her incessantly now ...*

Even Elisabeth's family is becoming more concerned about the melancholic empress. In 1897 her daughter Marie Valerie writes in her diary: *Sadly mum wants to be alone more than ever before ... and speaks only of sad things;* and in May 1898: *... the deep sadness which used to descend on mum only for periods at a time, now no longer leaves her. Mum said again today that she often longs for death ...*

Empress Elisabeth; retouched photograph from around 1897 from a photograph by Ludwig Angerer, 1863/64.

*I wished for my soul to escape to heaven
through a tiny hole in my heart.*

Elisabeth to baroness Rothschild on the day before her death

THE ASSASSINATION

In September 1898 Elisabeth stays several weeks in Territet near Montreux from where she makes numerous excursions. On 9th September Elisabeth and her lady-in-waiting Irma Sztáray take the steamship from

Caux to Geneva over Lake Geneva and from there with the carriage to Prégny to visit Baroness Rothschild. The Baroness's estate, including private moorings, lies directly on the lakeside. She offered to pick up Elisabeth with her yacht but Elisabeth declines politely because she would like to spend the evening in Geneva. After her enjoyable visit to Julie Rothschild, Elisabeth travels back to Geneva and stays in the Hotel Beau Rivage as always, under her pseudonym Countess of Hohenembs. In the evening she goes for a walk through the city with Irma Sztáray, she buys ice cream, buys a gift for Marie Valerie and returns to the hotel at about 10pm. Despite this

From the empress's travel albums: The ship's mooring in Geneva (above) and baroness Julie von Rothschild's estate in Prégny (below).

precaution, a Geneva newspaper reports the following day that the empress of Austria is staying in the . The report was also read by Luigi Lucheni, an Italian anarchist, who actually came to Geneva to murder the prince of Orléans. It did not bother Lucheni in the slightest that the prince

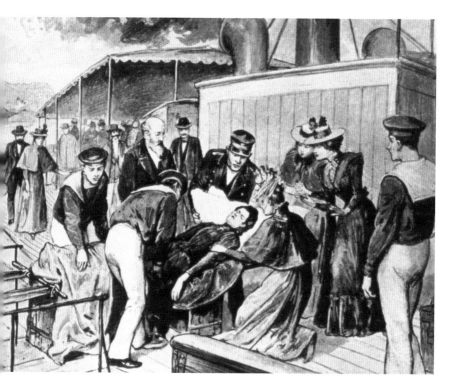

Above: The empress
collapses on board
the ship.

Previous page:
The last photograph of
the empress before her
death, together with Irma
Gräfin Sztáray, taken
on 3rd September 1898
in Territet.

had changed his travel route at the last moment and had left Geneva earlier than planned – by pure chance he now had a much more prominent victim in his sights.

The next morning, on 10th September, Elisabeth goes shopping, returns to the hotel and gets ready for the 13.40 ship to Caux. On the way to the mooring area, Luccheni lunges at the empress and drives a sharpened triangular file into her breast. Elisabeth falls to the ground but gets back up again thinking that nothing was amiss and thanks the passers-by who had rushed to her aid. Nobody, not even Elisabeth, notices the fatal injury. Luccheni had stabbed the empress in the middle of the heart and she was suffering from internal bleeding. Both ladies go on board the ship. No sooner do they board when Elisabeth collapses. Eau de Cologne and sugar dipped in ether were used to try and revive her.

Elisabeth sits up again, thanks everybody and asks *Just what happened to me?* She then slumps backwards, unconscious. When Irma Sztáray then opens up the dress she discovers a small brownish stain on the batiste shirt, then the tiny stab wound, which is not bleeding. It is now that she realizes

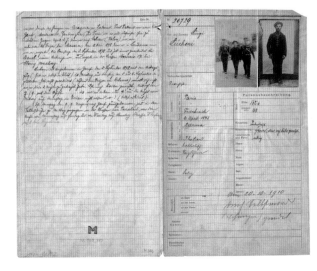

Above: Luigi Luccheni's interrogation document.

Left: The assassination weapon: a triangular file with wooden grip.

Elisabeth is fatally wounded. The ship returns to shore immediately and the dying empress is taken to her hotel room. At 14.40 the doctors can only pronounce her dead.

Marie Valerie writes in her diary: *So it has come just as she always wanted it, quick, painless, without medical treatment and without long, anxious days of worry for her loved ones.*

And when Franz Joseph hears the news from Count Paar, his Adjutant-General, his only words are: *You do not know how much I loved that woman.*

THE FUNERAL

Elisabeth's body is brought to Vienna and laid out in the chapel. The funeral ceremony takes place in the crypt of the Capuchin Church on 17th September. The sympathy of the people is expressed for the emperor as the victim of yet another heavy blow of fate. Count Kielmannsegg remarked later soberly: *Not many bemoan the loss of her.*

But Elisabeth's tragic death marks the beginning of her immortality and all criticism is forgotten. What remains is the memory of the beautiful and unapproachable empress.

The Sisi myth is born.

Above: Reports in the Vienna papers on the death of the empress.
Below: The empress's funeral cortege leaves the Hofburg.

Opposite page:
Above: Emperor Franz Joseph at the empress's coffin in the Hofburg; xylography, 1898.
Below: The empress's will.

Der Leichenzug verlässt die Hofburg.

Die feierliche Bestattung weil. Kaiserin Elisabeth in Wien.

Epilogue

Immediately after the crime, Luigi Lucheni tried to flee and threw away the file, breaking off the tip. But after just a few metres he was restrained and arrested. It was not until much later when the people heard of the fatal injury to Elisabeth that a search began for the inconspicuous file - and was located. Exactly one month after the assassination, Lucheni stood in court and proudly confessed to the murder, stating with gratification the huge interest in his trial and his notoriety. The verdict was life imprisonment and Lucheni was disappointed that the trial had been conducted under the Geneva judicial system since he could not be given the death sentence. Twelve years later, in October 1910, Lucheni hung himself in his cell with his leather belt.

In 1984, and under orders for utmost secrecy, the preserved remains of Lucheni were transferred to the Federal Pathologic-Anatomical Museum in Vienna, in the Narrenturm (Fools tower) of the old general hospital. Since the dissected head was not a scientifically analysable compound, and to prevent any sensationalism, Luigi Lucheni was cremated in the central cemetery in complete silence in 2002.

Opposite page: Silhouette of Empress Elisabeth. Design by Rolf Langenfass, 2001.

Sources

The Swiss Federal Archive, Bern. Literary remains of Empress Elisabeth of Austria, J I. 64

Austrian State Archives, House, Court and State archive Vienna. Egon Caesar Conte Corti, remaining material for Elisabeth's biography

Schloss Schönbrunn Kultur- und Betriebsges.m.b.H. Diary of Leopold Alram, Empress Elisabeth's footman

Bibliography

Brigitte Hamann, *Elisabeth. Kaiserin wider Willen,* Wien–München 1981

Brigitte Hamann, *Kaiserin Elisabeth. Das poetische Tagebuch,* Wien 1995

Brigitte Hamann, Elisabeth Hassmann, *Elisabeth. Stationen ihres Lebens,* Wien 1998

Egon Caesar Conte Corti, *Elisabeth. »Die seltsame Frau«,* Salzburg–Graz 1941

Verena von der Heyden-Rynsch (Hg.), *Elisabeth von Österreich. Tagebuchblätter von Constantin Christomanos,* München 1983

Georg Nostitz-Rieneck, *Briefe Kaiser Franz Josephs an Kaiserin Elisabeth,* 2 Bde., Wien 1966

Ingrid Haslinger, *Tafeln mit Sisi. Rezepte und Eßgewohnheiten der Kaiserin Elisabeth von Österreich,* Wien 1998

Franz Schnürer, *Briefe Kaiser Franz Josephs I. an seine Mutter 1838–1872,* München 1930

Irma Gräfin Sztáray, *Aus den letzten Jahren der Kaiserin Elisabeth,* Wien 1909

Marie Wallersee-Larisch, *Kaiserin Elisabeth und ich,* Leipzig 1935

Maria Freiin von Wallersee, *Meine Vergangenheit,* Berlin 1913

Gerda Mraz, Ulla Fischer-Westhauser, *Elisabeth. Wunschbilder oder Die Kunst der Retouche,* Wien 1998

Elisabeth von Österreich, Katalog zur Ausstellung des Historischen Museums der Stadt Wien, Hermesvilla, Wien 1986

Martha und Horst Schad, *Marie Valérie. Das Tagebuch der Lieblingstochter von Kaiserin Elisabeth von Österreich,* München 1998

Santo Cappon (Hg.), *Luigi Luccheni. »Ich bereue nichts!« Die Aufzeichnungen des Sisi-Mörders,* Wien 1998

Alphonse de Sondheimer, *Vitrine XIII. Geschichte und Schicksal der österreichischen Kronjuwelen,* Wien 1966

Chris Stadtlaender, *Sisi. Die geheimen Schönheitsrezepte der Kaiserin und des Hofes,* Wien 1995

Ingrid Haslinger, Katrin Unterreiner, *Kaiserappartements, Sisi Museum, Silberkammer. Die Residenz der Kaiserin Elisabeth,* Wien 2004

Technisches Museum Wien (Hg.), *Der Hofsalonwagen der Kaiserin Elisabeth,* Wien 2002

Bibliographic information published by the Deutsche Nationalbibliothek
The Deutsche Nationalbibliothek lists this publication in the Deutsche Nationalbibliografie;
detailed bibliographic data are available in the Internet at http://dnb.d-nb.de.

2nd edition 2006

Cover design: Christian Brandstätter
Editing, producing and layout: Barbara Sternthal
Reproduction of the images: Pixelstorm, Vienna,
Printing and binding: DELO tiskarna, Ljubljana.

ISBN 3-85498-416-2

Christian Brandstätter Verlag GmbH & Co KG
A-1080 Wien, Wickenburggasse 26
Telephone (+43-1) 512 15 43-0
Fax (+43-1) 512 15 43-231
E-Mail: info@cbv.at
www.cbv.at